AUSTRALIAN WILDLIFE

AUSTRALIAN WILDLIFE

FROM CROCODILES TO KANGAROOS, THE ICONIC ANIMALS OF THE ISLAND CONTINENT

NH
NEW
HOLLAND

THE UNIQUE WILDLIFE OF AUSTRALIA

A huge island continent separated from most other land masses by significant stretches of ocean for millions of years has meant that many unique species of animals have evolved in Australia and now call it home. These circumstances have enabled families such as marsupials to proliferate and fill many of the ecological niches which are occupied by other animal families elsewhere in the world. For example, we see many different species of kangaroos and wallabies living in habitats as varied as open plains, heathlands, rocky areas and dense forests, both on the ground and even up trees. Other branches of the marsupial family tree include carnivores, rodent-like species, possums, gliders, wombats, koalas and even marsupial 'moles'.

The likes of birds have many unique Australian species and even families, including lyrebirds, pardalotes and a huge diversity of parrots and honeyeaters, while the herpetofauna is incredibly rich. Australia is home to approximately 400 species of mammals, 950 birds, 1,000 reptiles, 240 frogs, 8,500 spiders and many tens of thousands of insects. A significant proportion of each group are endemic, meaning that they are found nowhere else on the planet.

The size and geography of Australia have facilitated this diversity and it is home to a broad range of habitats, including many different kinds of deserts, forests, grasslands, heathlands and mountain ranges, while offshore marine habitats are no less varied and include coral reefs and kelp forests among the most significant. This book is a celebration of the magnificent wildlife Australia has to offer, revealing a snapshot covering its huge and wonderful array of life forms.

MAMMALS

Short-beaked Echidna (*Tachyglossus aculeatus*)

Platypus (*Ornithorhynchus anatinus*)

Western Quoll (*Dasyurus geoffroii*)

Southern Ningaui (*Ningaui yvonneae*)

Yellow-footed Antechinus (*Antechinus flavipes*)

Slender-tailed Dunnart (*Sminthopsis murina*)

Fat-tailed Dunnart (*Sminthopsis crassicaudata*)

Brown Antechinus (*Antechinus stuartii*)

Brush-tailed Phascogale (*Phascogale tapoatafa*)

Kultarr (*Antechinomys laniger*)

Narrow-nosed Planigale (*Planigale tenuirostris*)

Northern Brown Bandicoot (*Isoodon macrourus*)

Numbat (*Myrmecobius fasciatus*)

Tasmanian Devil (*Sarcophilus harrisii*)

Southern Brown Bandicoot (*Isoodon obesulus*)

Bilby (*Macrotis lagotis*)

Northern Hairy-nosed Wombat (*Lasiorhinus krefftii*)

Southern Hairy-nosed Wombat (*Lasiorhinus latifrons*)

Common Wombat (*Vombatus ursinus*)

Koala (*Phascolarctos cinereus*)

Western Pygmy-Possum (*Cercartetus concinnus*)

Common Brushtail Possum (*Trichosurus vulpecula*)

Sugar Glider (*Petaurus breviceps*)

Yellow-bellied Glider (*Petaurus australis*)

Squirrel Glider (*Petaurus norfolcensis*)

Common Ringtail Possum (*Pseudocheirus peregrinus*)

Narrow-toed Feathertail Glider (*Acrobates pygmaeus*)

Green Ringtail Possum (*Pseudochirops archeri*)

Musky Rat-Kangaroo (*Hypsiprymnodon moschatus*)

Rufous Bettong (*Aepyprymnus rufescens*)

Woylie (*Bettongia penicillata*)

Long-nosed Potoroo (*Potorous tridactylus*)

Honey Possum (*Tarsipes rostratus*)

Yellow-footed Rock-Wallaby (*Petrogale xanthopus*)

Spectacled Hare-Wallaby (*Lagorchestes conspicillatus*)

Western Grey Kangaroo (*Macropus fuliginosus*)

Eastern Grey Kangaroo (*Macropus giganteus*)

Lumholtz's Tree-Kangaroo (*Dendrolagus lumholtzi*)

Tammar Wallaby (*Notamacropus eugenii*)

Parma Wallaby (*Notamacropus parma*)

Whiptail Wallaby (*Notamacropus parryi*)

Northern Nailtail Wallaby (*Onychogalea unguifera*)

Red Kangaroo (*Osphranter rufus*)

Allied Rock-Wallaby (*Petrogale assimilis*)

Nabarlek (*Petrogale concinna*)

Red-legged Pademelon (*Thylogale stigmatica*)

Swamp Wallaby (*Wallabia bicolor*)

Quokka (*Setonix brachyurus*)

Red-necked Pademelon (*Thylogale thetis*)

Northern Blossom Bat (*Macroglossus minimus*)

Grey-headed Flying-fox (*Pteropus poliocephalus*)

Ghost Bat (*Macroderma gigas*)

Dusky Leaf-nosed Bat (*Hipposideros ater*)

Common Bent-wing Bat (*Miniopterus schreibersii*)

Water Rat (*Hydromys chrysogaster*)

Spinifex Hopping Mouse (Notomys alexis)

Common Rock Rat (*Zyzomys argurus*)

Dugong (*Dugong dugon*)

Australian Sea-lion (*Neophoca cinerea*)

Australian Fur Seal (*Arctocephalus pusillus*)

Dingo (*Canis lupus dingo*)

Southern Right Whale (Eubalaena australis)

Dwarf Minke Whale (*Balaenoptera acutorostrata*)

Humpback Whale (*Megaptera novaeangliae*)

Indo-Pacific Bottlenose Dolphin (*Tursiops aduncus*)

Common Dolphin (*Delphinus delphis*)

Fraser's Dolphin (*Lagenodelphis hosei*)

BIRDS

Southern Cassowary (*Casuarius casuarius*)

Emu (*Dromaius novaehollandiae*)

Magpie Goose (Anseranas semipalmata)

Black Swan (*Cygnus atratus*)

Australian Shelduck (*Tadorna tadornoides*)

Australian Wood Duck (*Chenonetta jubata*)

Musk Duck (*Biziura lobata*)

Malleefowl (*Leipoa ocellata*)

Brown Quail (*Coturnix ypsilophora*)

Australasian Grebe (*Tachybaptus novaehollandiae*)

Crested Pigeon (*Ocyphaps lophotes*)

Common Bronzewing (*Phaps chalcoptera*)

Australian Bustard (*Ardeotis australis*)

Fan-tailed Cuckoo (*Cacomantis flabelliformis*)

Tawny Frogmouth (*Podargus strigoides*)

Large-tailed Nightjar (*Caprimulgus macrurus*)

95

Australian Owlet-nightjar (*Aegotheles cristatus*)

Brolga (*Antigone rubicunda*)

Buff-banded Rail (*Gallirallus philippensis*)

Australian Crake (*Porzana fluminea*)

Dusky Moorhen (*Gallinula tenebrosa*)

Australasian Swamphen (*Porphyrio melanotus*)

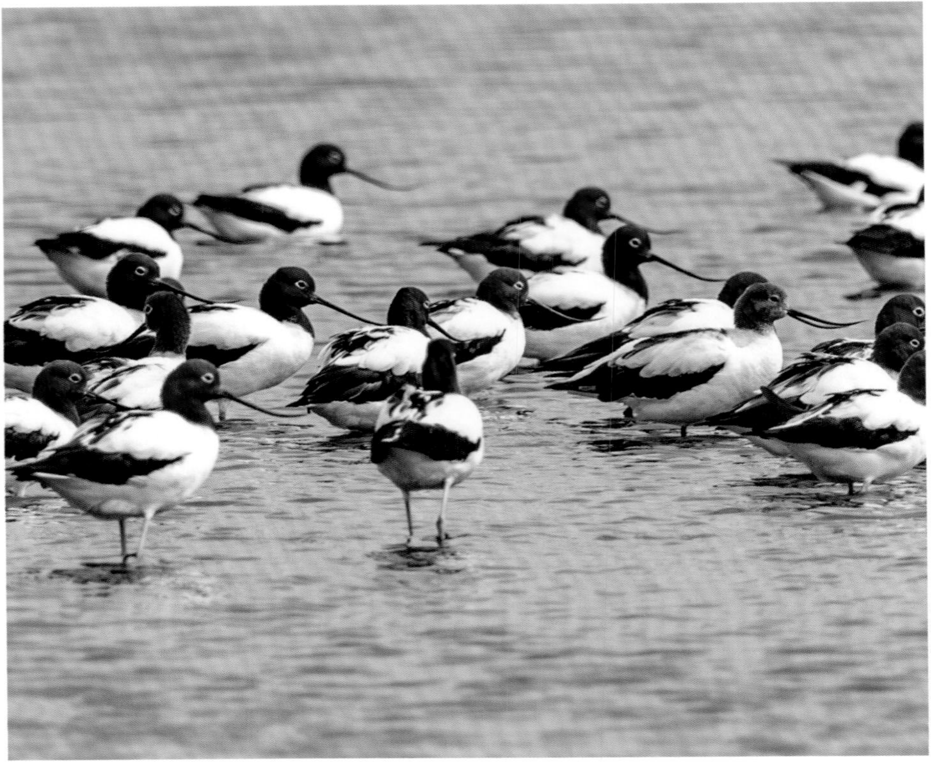

Red-necked Avocet (*Recurvirostra novaehollandiae*)

Pied Oystercatcher (*Haematopus longirostris*)

Grey Plover (*Pluvialis squatarola*)

Red-capped Plover (*Charadrius ruficapillus*)

Plains-wanderer (*Pedionomus torquatus*)

Comb-crested Jacana (*Irediparra gallinacea*)

Hooded Plover (*Thinornis cucullatus*)

Bar-tailed Godwit (*Limosa lapponica*)

Curlew Sandpiper (*Calidris ferruginea*)

Terek Sandpiper (*Xenus cinereus*)

Common Sandpiper (*Actitis hypoleucos*)

Painted Buttonquail (*Turnix varius*)

Australian Pratincole (*Stiltia isabella*)

Fairy Tern (*Sternula nereis*)

Silver Gull (*Chroicocephalus novaehollandiae*)

Black-browed Albatross (*Thalassarche melanophris*)

Little Penguin (*Eudyptula novaehollandiae*)

Wilson's Storm-Petrel (*Oceanites oceanicus*)

Cook's Petrel (*Pterodroma cookii*)

Australasian Darter (*Anhinga novaehollandiae*)

Black-necked Stork (Ephippiorhynchus asiaticus)

Brown Booby (*Sula leucogaster*)

Great Frigatebird (*Fregata minor*)

Australian Pelican (*Pelecanus conspicillatus*)

White-faced Heron (*Egretta novaehollandiae*)

Australian Ibis (*Threskiornis moluccus*)

Royal Spoonbill (*Platalea regia*)

Yellow-billed Spoonbill (*Platalea flavipes*)

Osprey (*Pandion haliaetus*)

Black-shouldered Kite (*Elanus axillaris*)

Wedge-tailed Eagle (*Aquila audax*)

Noisy Pitta (*Pitta versicolor*)

Rufous Owl (*Ninox rufa*)

Southern Boobook (*Ninox boobook*)

Azure Kingfisher (*Ceyx azureus*)

Forest Kingfisher (*Todiramphus macleayii*)

Rainbow Bee-eater (*Merops ornatus*)

Laughing Kookaburra (*Dacelo novaeguineae*)

Dollarbird (*Eurystomus orientalis*)

Peregrine Falcon (*Falco peregrinus*)

Red-tailed Black-Cockatoo (*Calyptorhynchus banksii*)

Gang-gang Cockatoo (*Callocephalon fimbriatum*)

Pink Cockatoo (*Lophochroa leadbeateri*)

145

Galah (*Eolophus roseicapilla*)

Little Corella (*Cacatua sanguinea*)

Australian King-Parrot (*Alisterus scapularis*)

Sulphur-crested Cockatoo (*Cacatua galerita*)

Mulga Parrot (*Psephotellus varius*)

Ground Parrot (*Pezoporus wallicus*)

Australian Ringneck (*Barnardius zonarius*)

Eastern Rosella (*Platycercus eximius*)

Musk Lorikeet (*Glossopsitta concinna*)

Budgerigar (*Melopsittacus undulatus*)

Rainbow Lorikeet (*Trichoglossus moluccanus*)

Superb Lyrebird (*Menura novaehollandiae*)

Spotted Catbird (*Ailuroedus maculosus*)

Regent Bowerbird (*Sericulus chrysocephalus*)

Satin Bowerbird (*Ptilonorhynchus violaceus*)

Brown Treecreeper (*Climacteris picumnus*)

Western Grasswren (*Amytornis textilis*)

Southern Emu-wren (*Stipiturus malachurus*)

Blue-breasted Fairy-wren (*Malurus pulcherrimus*)

Superb Fairy-wren (*Malurus cyaneus*)

Eastern Spinebill (*Acanthorhynchus tenuirostris*)

Noisy Miner (*Manorina melanocephala*)

Lewin's Honeyeater (*Meliphaga lewinii*)

Regent Honeyeater (*Anthochaera phrygia*)

Crimson Chat (*Epthianura tricolor*)

Scarlet Honeyeater (*Myzomela sanguinolenta*)

New Holland Honeyeater (*Phylidonyris novaehollandiae*)

Spotted Pardalote (*Pardalotus punctatus*)

Western Bristlebird (*Dasyornis longirostris*)

Rockwarbler (*Origma solitaria*)

Yellow-throated Scrubwren (*Neosericornis citreogularis*)

White-browed Scrubwren (*Sericornis frontalis*)

Inland Thornbill (*Acanthiza apicalis*)

White-throated Gerygone (*Gerygone olivacea*)

Crested Bellbird (*Oreoica gutturalis*)

Grey-crowned Babbler (*Pomatostomus temporalis*)

Australian Logrunner (*Orthonyx temminckii*)

Copper-backed Quail-thrush (*Cinclosoma clarum*)

Barred Cuckooshrike (*Coracina lineata*)

Varied Sittella (*Daphoenositta chrysoptera*)

Eastern Whipbird (*Psophodes olivaceus*)

Golden Whistler (*Pachycephala pectoralis*)

Rufous Whistler (*Pachycephala rufiventris*)

Eastern Shrike-tit (*Falcunculus frontatus*)

Grey Shrikethrush (*Colluricincla harmonica*)

Green Oriole (*Oriolus flavocinctus*)

Australasian Figbird (*Sphecotheres vieilloti*)

Yellow-breasted Boatbill (*Macheirirhynchus flaviventer*)

Masked Woodswallow (*Artamus personatus*)

Pied Butcherbird (*Cracticus nigrogularis*)

Australian Magpie (*Gymnorhina tibicen*)

Pied Currawong (*Strepera graculina*)

Black Currawong (*Strepera fuliginosa*)

Willie-wagtail (*Rhipidura leucophrys*)

Spangled Drongo (*Dicrurus bracteatus*)

Victoria's Riflebird (*Ptiloris victoriae*)

Magnificent Riflebird (*Ptiloris magnificus*)

Paradise Riflebird (*Ptiloris paradiseus*)

Black-faced Monarch (*Monarcha melanopsis*)

Magpie-lark (*Grallina cyanoleuca*)

Satin Flycatcher (*Myiagra cyanoleuca*)

Apostlebird (*Struthidea cinerea*)

White-winged Chough (*Corcorax melanorhamphos*)

Australian Raven (*Corvus coronoides*)

Jacky-winter (*Microeca fascinans*)

Scarlet Robin (*Petroica boodang*)

Eastern Yellow Robin (*Eopsaltria australis*)

Grey-headed Robin (*Heteromyias cinereifrons*)

Silvereye (*Zosterops lateralis*)

Metallic Starling (*Aplonis metallica*)

Russet-tailed Thrush (*Zoothera heinei*)

Mistletoebird (*Dicaeum hirundinaceum*)

Olive-backed Sunbird (*Nectarinia jugularis*)

Diamond Firetail (*Stagonopleura guttata*)

Zebra Finch (*Taeniopygia guttata*)

REPTILES

Freshwater Crocodile (*Crocodylus johnstoni*)

Leatherback Turtle (*Dermochelys coriacea*)

Flatback Turtle (*Natator depressus*)

Green Turtle (*Chelonia mydas*)

Eastern Long-necked Turtle (*Chelodina longicollis*)

Pig-nosed Turtle (*Carettochelys insculpta*)

Common Thick-tailed Gecko (*Underwoodisaurus milii*)

Burton's Snake-Lizard (*Lialis burtonis*)

Eastern Bearded Dragon (*Pogona barbata*)

Lace Monitor (*Varanus varius*)

Western Blue-tongue Skink (*Tiliqua occipitalis*)

Green Python (*Morelia viridis*)

Brown Tree Snake (*Boiga irregularis*)

Common Death Adder (*Acanthophis antarcticus*)

Saltwater Crocodile (*Crocodylus porosus*)

Rough-throated Leaf-tailed Gecko (*Saltuarius salebrosus*)

Centralian Knob-tailed Gecko (*Nephrurus amyae*)

Eastern Deserts Fat-tailed Gecko (*Diplodactylus ameyi*)

Mesa Gecko (*Diplodactylus galeatus*)

Inland Marbled Velvet Gecko (*Oedura cincta*)

Golden-tailed Gecko (*Strophurus taenicauda*)

Copper-tailed Skink (*Ctenotus taeniolatus*)

Pink-tongue Skink (*Cyclodomorphus gerrardii*)

Mainland She-Oak Skink (*Cyclodomorphus michaeli*)

Shingleback (*Tiliqua rugosa*)

Frilled Lizard (*Chlamydosaurus kingii*)

251

Central Netted Dragon (*Ctenophorus nuchalis*)

Boyd's Forest Dragon (*Lophosaurus boydii*)

Water Dragon (*Intellagama lesueurii*)

Spiny-tailed Monitor (*Varanus acanthurus*)

Perentie (*Varanus giganteus*)

Stimson's Python (*Antaresia stimsoni*)

Woma (Aspidites ramsayi)

Rough-scaled Python (*Morelia carinata*)

Keelback (*Tropidonophis mairii*)

Highlands Copperhead (*Austrelaps ramsayi*)

Australian Coral Snake (*Brachyurophis australis*)

Golden-crowned Snake (*Cacophis squamulosus*)

Yellow-faced Whipsnake (*Demansia psammophis*)

Tiger Snake (*Notechis scutatus*)

Inland Taipan (*Oxyuranus microlepidotus*)

King Brown Snake (*Pseudechis australis*)

Yellow-bellied Sea Snake (*Hydrophis platurus*)

FROGS

Magnificent Tree Frog (*Litoria splendida*)

Green-and-golden Bell Frog (*Litoria aurea*)

Red-eyed Tree Frog (*Litoria chloris*)

Green Tree Frog (*Litoria caerulea*)

Southern Brown Tree Frog (*Litoria ewingii*)

Eastern Stony Creek Frog (*Litoria wilcoxii*)

Crucifix Frog (*Notaden bennettii*)

Striped Marsh Frog (*Limnodynastes peronii*)

Common Eastern Froglet (*Crinia signifera*)

Southern Corroboree Frog (*Pseudophryne corroboree*)

Red-backed Toadlet (*Pseudophryne coriacea*)

Red-crowned Toadlet (*Pseudophryne australis*)

FISHES

Pyjama Cardinalfish (*Sphaeramia nematoptera*)

Bumphead Parrotfish (*Bolbometopon muricatum*)

Azure Damselfish (*Chrysiptera hemicyanea*)

Weedy Seadragon (*Phyllopteryx taeniolatus*)

Pygmy Seahorse (*Hippocampus bargibanti*)

Leafy Seadragon (*Phycodurus eques*)

Zebra Moray (*Gymnomuraena zebra*)

Bull Shark (*Carcharhinus leucas*)

Great White Shark (*Carcharodon carcharias*)

Great Hammerhead (*Sphyrna mokarran*)

Queensland Groper (*Epinephelus lanceolatus*)

Emperor Angelfish (*Pomacanthus imperator*)

Mandarinfish (*Synchiropus splendidus*)

Tasselled Leatherjacket (*Chaetodermis penicilligerus*)

Port Jackson Shark (*Heterodontus portusjacksoni*)

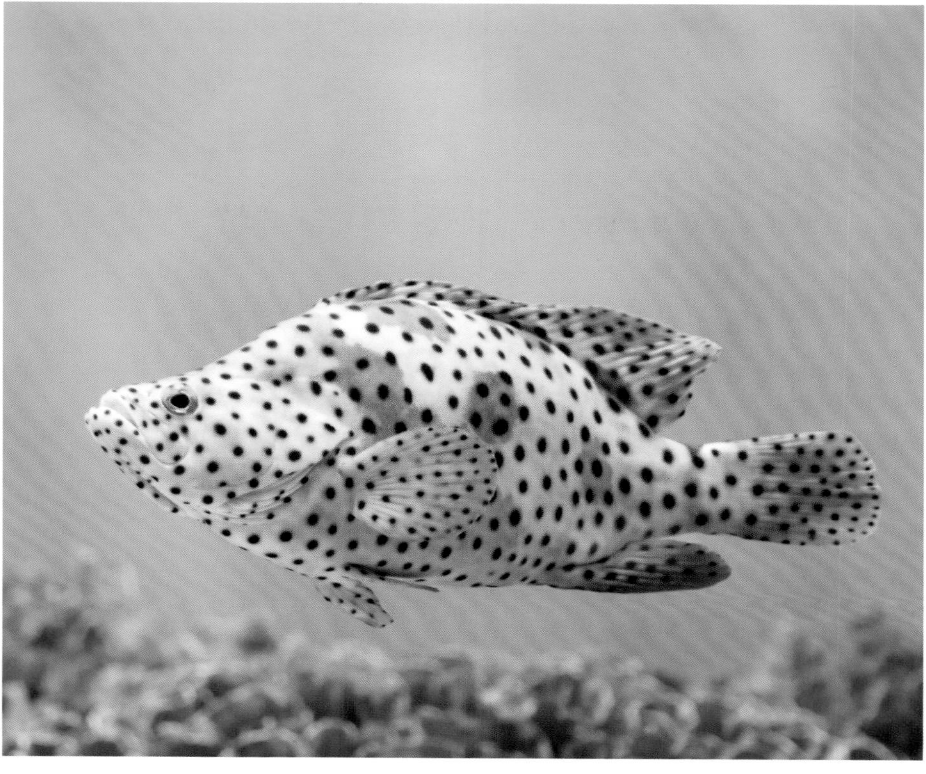

Barramundi Cod (*Cromileptes altivelis*)

Longnose Hawkfish (*Oxycirrhites typus*)

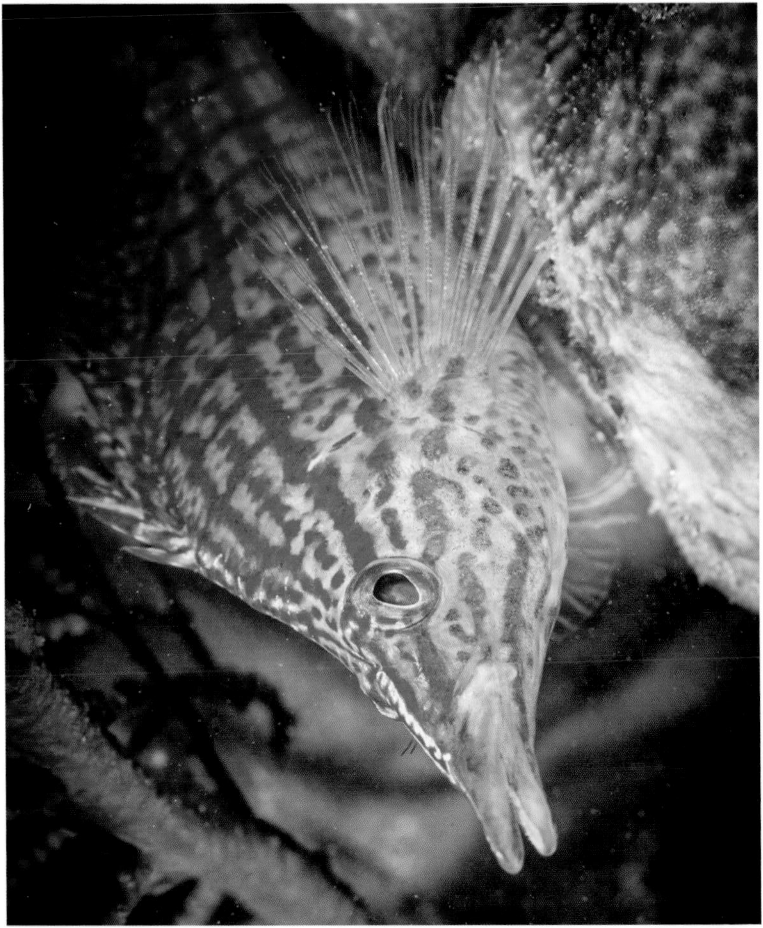

Clown Triggerfish (*Balistoides conspicillum*)

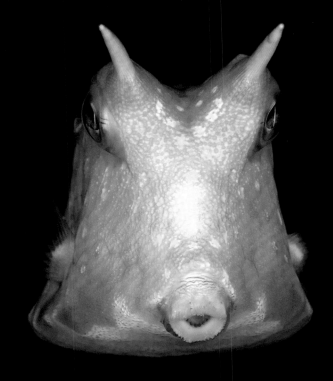

Longhorn Cowfish (*Lactoria cornuta*)

Longfin Batfish (*Platax pinnatus*)

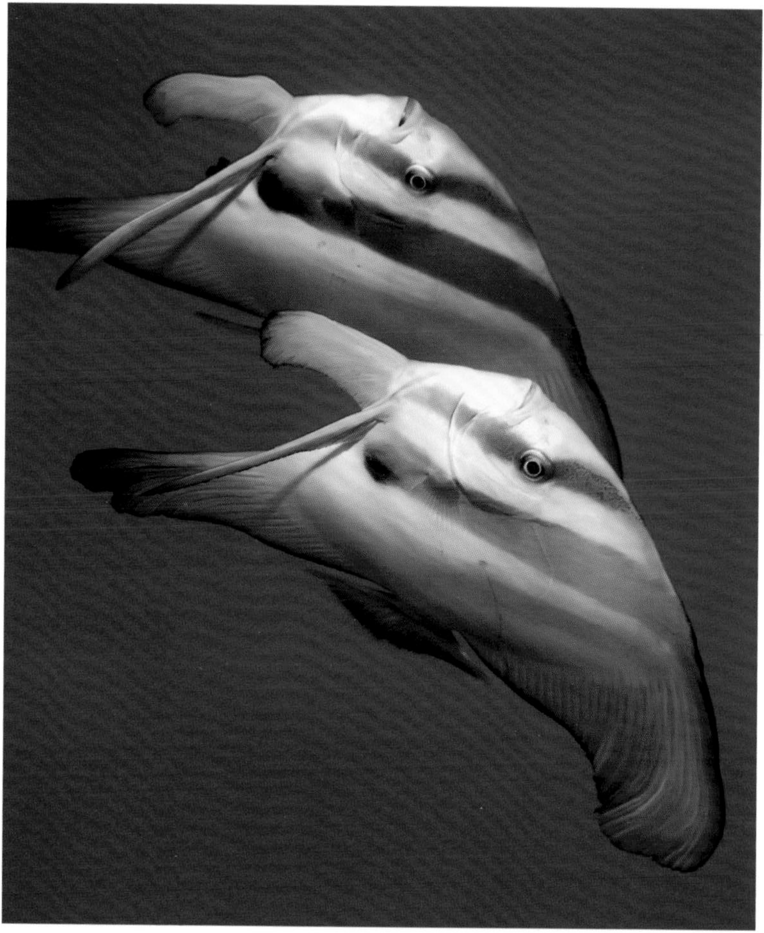

INVERTEBRATES

Sydney Funnel-web Spider (*Atrax robustus*)

Bull Ant (*Myrmecia* spp.)

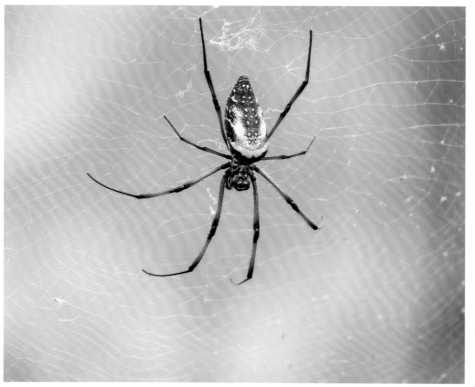

Giant Golden Orb-weaver (*Nephila pilipes*)

Hercules Moth (*Coscinocera hercules*)

Redback Spider (*Latrodectus hasselti*)

Goliath Stick Insect (*Eurycnema goliath*)

Giant Centipede (*Ethmostigmus rubripes*)

Giant Clam (*Tridacna gigas*)

Bigfin Reef Squid (*Sepioteuthis lessoniana*)

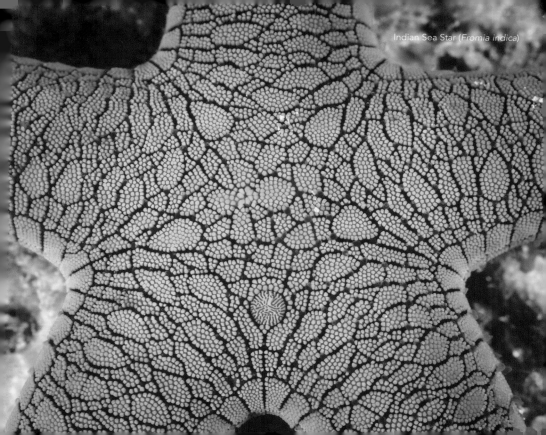

Indian Sea Star (*Fromia indica*)

Fiddler Crab (Ocypodidae)

St Andrew's Cross Spider (*Argiope keyserlingi*)

Australian Tarantula (*Selenotypus nebo*)

Net-casting Spider (*Deinopis subrufa*)

Peacock Jumping Spider (*Maratus volans*)

White Flower Spider (*Zygometis xanthogaster*)

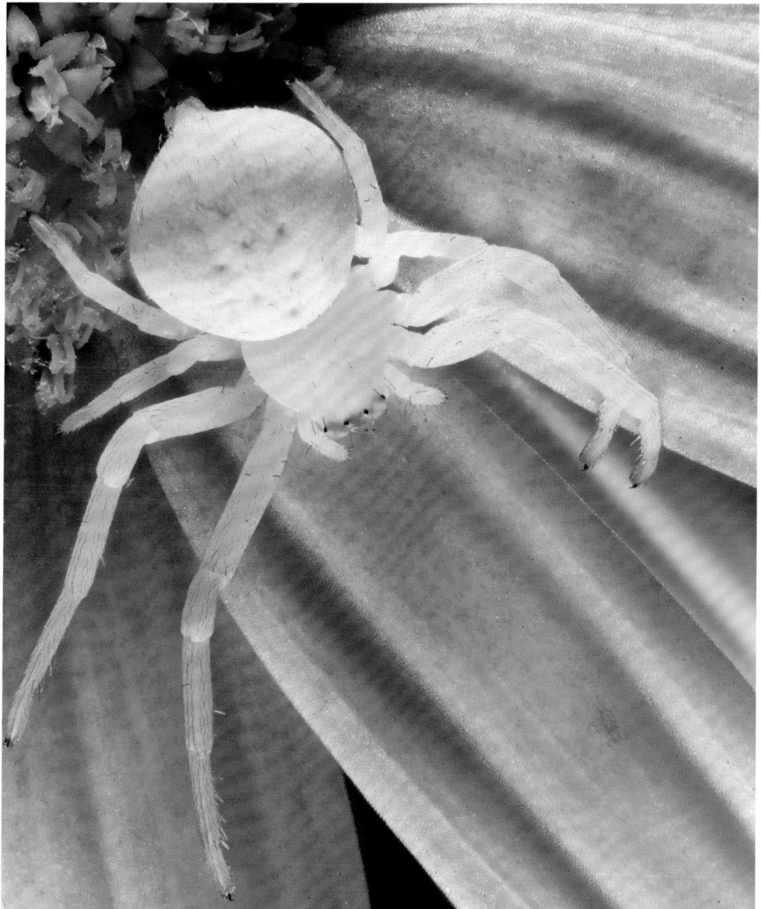

Orange Threadtail (*Nososticta solida*)

Common Flatwing (*Austroargiolestes icteromelas*)

Common Bluetail (*Ischnura heterosticta*)

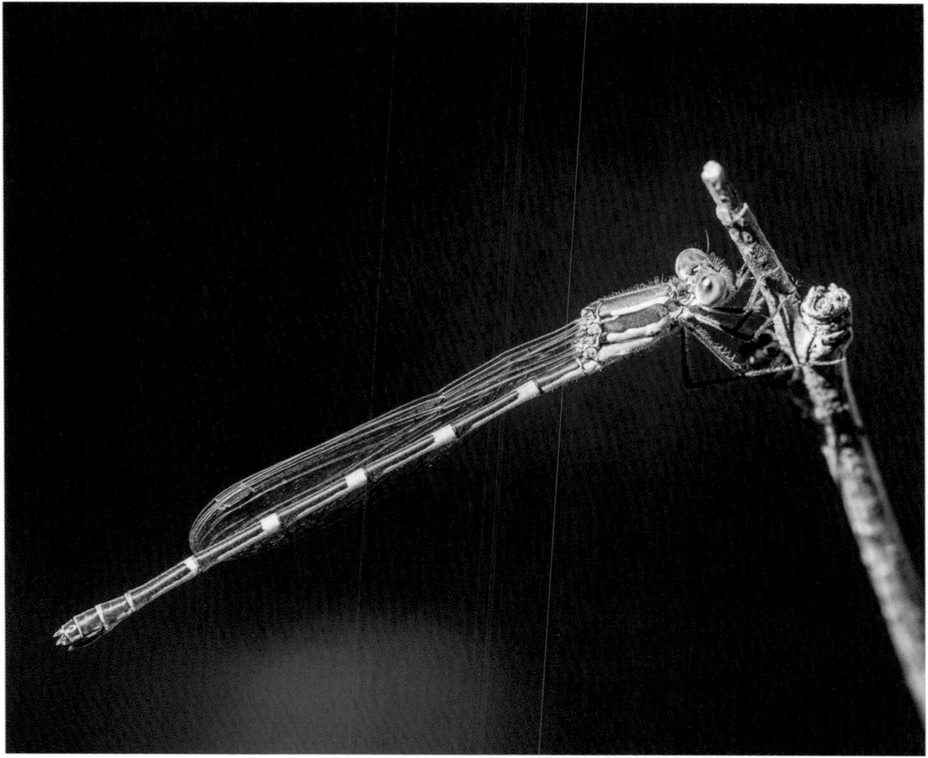

Slender Ringtail (*Austrolestes analis*)

Graphic Flutterer (*Rhyothemis graphiptera*)

Blue-spotted Hawker (*Adversaeschna brevistyla*)

Fiery Skimmer (*Orthetrum villosovittatum*)

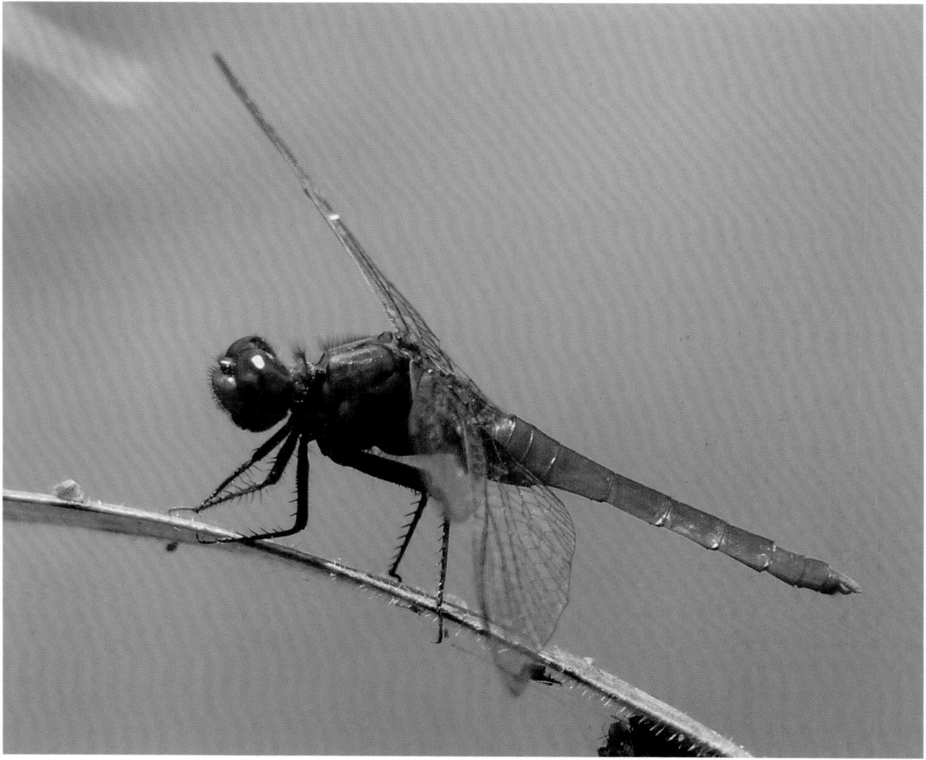

Red Arrow (*Rhodothemis lieftincki*)

Four O'Clock Moth (*Dysphania numana*)

Cairns Birdwing (*Ornithoptera euphorion*)

Green-spotted Triangle (*Graphium agamemnon*)

Orchard Swallowtail (*Papilio aegeus*)

Spotted Jezebel (*Delias aganippe*)

Wanderer (*Danaus plexippus*)

Common Eggfly (*Hypolimnas bolina*)

Meadow Argus (*Junonia villida*)

Splendid Ochre (*Trapezites symmomus*)

Bogong Moth (*Agrotis infusa*)

First published in 2024 by New Holland Publishers
Sydney

Level 1, 178 Fox Valley Road, Wahroonga, NSW 2076, Australia

newhollandpublishers.com

A record of this book is held at the National Library of Australia.

ISBN 9781760796365

Managing Director: Fiona Schultz
Designer: Andrew Davies
Production Director: Arlene Gippert
Printed in China

10 9 8 7 6 5 4 3 2 1

Keep up with New Holland Publishers:

 NewHollandPublishers

@newhollandpublishers